Meditations

MEDITATIONS

Dorothy Day

Selected & arranged by

Stanley Vishnewski

Drawings by Rita Corbin

TEMPLEGATE  PUBLISHERS

Originally published in 1970 by Newman Press

This edition © 1997 Tamar Hennessy

Templegate Publishers
302 East Adams Street
P.O. Box 5152
Springfield, IL
62705
(217) 522-3353
http://www.templegate.com

ISBN 0-87243-227-0
Library of Congress Catalog Number
97-60413

Contents

FOREWORD

The story is told in *The Catholic Worker* of how I first met Dorothy Day. During the dark days of the Great American Depression I supposedly went to Union Square to observe a Communist demonstration in progress. At the height of the activities I espied an old tired lady carrying a suitcase and typewriter. Gallantly I went up to her and politely inquired if I could be of any assistance — whereupon the old lady fixed me with a glance and said: "Follow me! I am about to start a newspaper."

That young man was then 17 and the tired old lady was 35 — but what amazed that young man even more was the fact that when he reached the age of 35 the tired old lady had grown considerably younger and more agile.

It is of such stories that legends are born. But in reality the meeting was more prosaic. In 1934, in my quest for work to do in Catholic Action, I found a copy of *The Catholic Worker* in the reading room of the public library. What I read there on those pages was an intimation of a glorious world to come. To me the words in the paper were an invitation and a challenge to do something to bring about a better social order based on the teachings of Christ. The crystal-clear message of *The Catholic Worker* touched me and impelled me to go and do likewise.

I was not the only one who had been touched by the message of *The Catholic Worker*, which was based on the teachings of the Gospels and the sublime doctrine of the Mystical Body of Christ. This doctrine was the underlying influence of much of the writings in the pages of *The Catholic Worker* and is reflected in these Meditations. It was the beautiful Pauline doctrine that we are all members of Christ and that what we do to the least we do to Christ. This inspired hundreds of young men and women to leave comfortable homes and spend years in the slums ministering to the victims of our society, providing a glorious chapter in the history of our Church that still remains to be written.

Reading through the pages of *The Catholic Worker* in an effort to cull some of Dorothy Day's writings that had made a deep impression upon us, I was greatly struck by the fact of how the awareness of the spiritual and of the doctrine of the Mystical Body of Christ inspires and animates the pages.

I have tried to bring together in these pages not the best of Dorothy Day's writings but what I consider to be the most representative of the thought of *The Catholic Worker*. It was a task I loved, for to go through the pages of *The Catholic Worker* was to relive the story of my life, since in a way I was present at the scene and took part in many of the activities that resulted in the composition of these Meditations.

It is with love and with nostalgia that I look back over the thirty-five years which were rich and full of adventure; for it is true that the greatest adventure of modern times is that of the spiritual life.

I have a fondness in my heart for that little store front at 436 East 15th Street in New York which housed the first editorial office of *The Catholic Worker*. It was there that I first met Dorothy Day, Peter Maurin, Mary Sheehan, Big Dan Orr, Little Dan, and the group of dedicated Catholics who had banded together to attempt to bring about a better social order based on the teachings of Christ.

What impressed me most was the dedication and the unfailing charity and love of the staff. Everyone who came to the store front was greeted as Christ, and all were invited to stay and break bread with the community. One quickly came to the realization that in Christ we formed but one family and that we were all brothers.

It was for this reason that we engaged in the class struggle, that we went out on the streets to sell our papers and to distribute our leaflets. We used to go to meetings, parades and demonstrations to distribute our leaflets, which were indeed short meditations on the teachings of the Church on war, labor and strikes, and hand them out to all. Many of them were torn up, and we were cursed and reviled. But we were young then, and we gloried in being accounted to be called fools for the love of Christ.

We can only know about what we have practiced, Dorothy once told me. Peter Maurin insisted that the purpose of *The Catholic Worker* was not to write about news but to create news. The pages of the paper began to reflect the manifold activities of the Catholic Workers. There was no attempt made at fine writing or to attain an exquisite style. The Meditations in the paper (reprinted in this book) were often written in snatches while engaged in the practical apostolate. They were written while cooking meals, taking care of babies, selling papers on the streets, walking the picket line, and participating in the other prosaic events that filled our days — but events, if only we had the faith to see and observe, that were filled with a deep spiritual significance. For it is only in the duties of the moment that we are able to see and find Christ.

Stanley Vishnewski
Catholic Worker Farm
Tivoli, New York

PRACTICAL MEDITATIONS

I know that what I write will be tinged with all the daily doings, with myself, my child, my work, my study, as well as with God. God enters into them all. He is inseparable from them. I think of Him as I wake and as I think of Teresa's daily doings. Perhaps it is that I have a wandering mind. But I do not care. It is a woman's mind, and if my daily written meditations are of the people about me, of what is going on — then it must be so. It is a part of every meditation to apply the virtue, the mystery, to the daily life we lead.

I shall meditate as I have been accustomed, in the little Italian Church on Twelfth Street, by the side of the open window, looking out at the plants growing on the roof, the sweet corn, the boxes of herbs, the geraniums in bright bloom, and I shall rest happy in the presence of Christ on the altar, and then I shall come home and I shall write, as Père Graty advises, and try to catch some of these things that happen to bring me nearer to God, to catch them and put them down on paper.

And because I am a woman involved in practical cares, I cannot give the first half of the day to these things, but must meditate when I can, early in the morning and on the fly during the day. Not in the privacy of a study — but here, there and everywhere — at the kitchen table, on the train, on the ferry, on my way to and from appointments and even while making supper or putting Teresa to bed.

House of Hospitality

13

CALIFORNIA EARTHQUAKE

What I remember most plainly about the earthquake was the human warmth and kindliness of everyone afterward. For days refugees poured out of burning San Francisco and camped in Idora Park and the race track in Oakland. People came in their night clothes; there were new-born babies.

Mother had always complained before about how clannish California people were, how if you were from the East they snubbed you and were loath to make friends. But after the earthquake everyone's heart was enlarged by Christian charity. All the hard crust of worldly reserve and prudence was shed. Each person was a little child in friendliness and warmth.

Mother and all our neighbors were busy from morning to night cooking hot meals. They gave away every extra garment they possessed. They stripped themselves to the bone in giving, forgetful of the morrow. While the crisis lasted, people loved each other. They realized their own helplessness while nature "travaileth and groaneth." It was as though they were united in Christian solidarity. It makes one think of how people could, if they would, care for each other in time of stress, unjudgingly, with pity and with love.

From Union Square to Rome

FIRST IMPULSE TOWARDS CATHOLICISM

It was Mrs. Barrett who gave me my first impulse towards Catholicism. It was around ten o'clock in the morning that I went up to Kathryn's to call for her to come out and play. There was no one on the porch or in the kitchen. The breakfast dishes had all been washed. They were long railroad apartments, those flats, and thinking the children must be in the front room, I burst in and ran through the bedrooms.

In the front room Mrs. Barrett was on her knees, saying her prayers. She turned to tell me that Kathryn and the children had all gone to the store and went on with her praying. And I felt a warm burst of love towards Mrs. Barrett that I have never forgotten, a feeling of gratitude and happiness that still warms my heart when I remember her. She had God, and there was beauty and joy in her life.

All through my life what she was doing remained with me. And though I became oppressed with the problem of poverty and injustice, though I groaned at the hideous sordidness of man's lot, though there were years when I clung to the philosophy of economic determination as an explanation of man's fate, still there were moments when in the midst of misery and class strife, life was shot through with glory. Mrs. Barrett in her sordid little tenement flat finished her breakfast dishes at ten o'clock in the morning and got down on her knees and prayed to God.

From Union Square to Rome

SOLITARY CONFINEMENT

All through those weary first days in jail when I was in solitary confinement, the only thoughts that brought comfort to my soul were those lines in the Psalms that expressed the terror and misery of man suddenly stricken and abandoned. Solitude and hunger and weariness of spirit — these sharpened my perceptions so that I suffered not only my own sorrow but the sorrows of those about me. I was no longer myself. I was man. I was no longer a young girl, part of a radical movement seeking justice for those oppressed. I was the oppressed. I was that drug addict, screaming and tossing in her cell, beating her head against the wall. I was that shoplifter who for rebellion was sentenced to solitary. I was that woman who had killed her children, who had murdered her lover.

The blackness of hell was all about me. The sorrows of the world encompassed me. I was like one gone down into the pit. Hope had forsaken me. I was that mother whose child had been raped and slain. I was the mother who had borne the monster who had done it. I was even that monster, feeling in my own heart every abomination.

From Union Square to Rome

HOUND OF HEAVEN

It was on one of those cold, bitter winter evenings that I first heard *The Hound of Heaven,* that magnificent poem of Francis Thompson. Gene could recite all of it, and he used to sit there, looking dour and black, his head sunk on his chest, sighing, "And now my heart is as a broken fount wherein tear-drippings stagnate." It is one of those poems that awakens the soul, recalls it to the fact that God is its destiny. The idea of this pursuit fascinated me; the inevitableness of it, the recurrence of it, made me feel that inescapably I would have to pause in the mad rush of living to remember my first beginning and last end.

From Union Square to Rome

EARLY MASS

You will be surprised but there was many a morning after sitting all night in taverns or coming from balls over at Webster Hall that I went to an early Mass at St. Joseph's Church on Sixth Avenue. It was just around the corner from where I lived, and seeing people going to an early weekday Mass attracted me. What were they finding there? I seemed to feel the faith of those about me and I longed for their faith. My own life was sordid and yet I had had occasional glimpses of the true and the beautiful. So I used to go in and kneel in a back pew of St. Joseph's, and perhaps I asked even then, "God, be merciful to me, a sinner."

From Union Square to Rome

NEW LIFE

My child was born in March at the end of a harsh winter. In December I had to come in from the country and take a little apartment in town. It was good to be there, close to friends, close to a church where I could stop and pray. I read the *Imitation of Christ* a great deal. I knew that I was going to have my child baptized a Catholic, cost what it may. I knew that I was not going to have her floundering through many years as I had done, doubting and hesitating, undisciplined and amoral. I felt it was the greatest thing I could do for a child. For myself, I prayed for the gift of faith. I was sure, yet not sure. I postponed the day of decision.

A woman does not want to be alone at such a time. Even the most hardened, the most irreverent, is awed by the stupendous fact of creation. No matter how cynically or casually the worldly may treat the birth of a child, it remains spiritually and physically a tremendous event. God pity the woman who does not feel the fear, the awe, and the joy of bringing a child into the world.

From Union Square to Rome

TERESA WAS BAPTIZED

Finally the great day arrived and was a thing of the past. Teresa was baptized; she had become a member of the Mystical Body of Christ. I didn't know anything of the Mystical Body or I might have felt disturbed at being separated from her.

But I clutched her close to me, and all that summer as I nursed her and bent over that tiny round face at my breast, I was filled with a deep happiness that nothing could spoil. But the obstacles to my becoming a Catholic were there, shadows in the background of my life.

I had become convinced that I would become a Catholic, and yet I felt I was betraying the class to which I belonged, you my brother, the workers, the poor of the world, the class which Christ most loved and spent his life with.

From Union Square to Rome

BAPTISM

It was in December, 1927, a most miserable day, and the trip was long from the city down to Tottenville, Staten Island. All the way on the ferry through the foggy bay I felt grimly that I was being too precipitate. I had no sense of peace, no joy, no conviction even that what I was doing was right. It was just something that I had to do, a task to be gotten through. I doubted myself when I allowed myself to think. I hated myself for being weak and vacillating. A most consuming restlessness was upon me so that I walked around and around the deck of the ferry, almost groaning in anguish of spirit. Perhaps the devil was on the boat.

Sister Aloysia was there waiting for me, to be my godmother. I do not know whether I had any other godparent. Father Hyland, gently, with reserve, with matter-of-factness, heard my confession and baptized me.

I was a Catholic at last though at that moment I never felt less the joy and peace and consolation which I know from my own later experiences religion can bring.

A year later my confirmation was indeed joyful and Pentecost never passes without a renewed sense of happiness and thanksgiving. It was only then that the feeling of uncertainty finally left me, never again to return, praise God!

From Union Square to Rome

21

CHRIST'S POOR

I watched that ragged horde and thought to myself, that these are Christ's poor. He was one of them. He was a man like other men, and He chose His friends amongst the ordinary workers. These men feel they have been betrayed by Christianity. Men are not Christian today. If they were, this sight would not be possible. Far dearer in the sight of God perhaps are these hungry ragged ones, than all those smug, well-fed Christians who sit in their homes, cowering in fear of the Communist menace.

I felt that they were my people, that I was part of them. I had worked for them and with them in the past, and now I was a Catholic and so could not be a Communist. I could not join this united front of protest and I wanted to.

The feast of the Immaculate Conception was the next day and I went out to the National Shrine and assisted at solemn high Mass there. There I offered up a special prayer, a prayer which came with tears and anguish, that some way would open up for me to use what talents I possessed for my fellow workers, for the poor and the oppressed.

When I got back to New York, Peter Maurin was at the house waiting for me.

House of Hospitality

PETER MAURIN

When I first saw Peter Maurin my impression was of a short, broad-shouldered workingman with a high, broad head covered with greying hair. His face was weatherbeaten, he had warm grey eyes and a wide pleasant mouth. The collar of his shirt was dirty, but he had tried to dress up by wearing a tie and a suit which looked as though he had slept in it. (As I found out afterward, indeed he had.)

What struck me first about him was that he was one of those people who talked you deaf, dumb and blind, who each time he saw you began his conversation just where he had left off at the previous meeting, and never stopped unless you begged for rest, and that was not for long. He was irrepressible and he was incapable of taking offense.

At that time Peter Maurin was fifty-seven, had never married, had been "away from the Church" in his youth, had worked with Sangnier and his social studies group in Paris, and had sold its paper, *Le Sillon* (The Furrow). He believed in going to the people in town and countryside, because first of all he was of the people himself. He was born in a tiny hamlet in the southern part of France, two-hundred miles from Barcelona, one of a family of twenty-four children. His own mother had died after she had borne her fifth child, and his stepmother had had nineteen and was still alive, he said.

Jubilee

FAITH OF PETER

Peter's idea of hospices seemed a simple and logical one to me; hospices such as they had in the Middle Ages certainly were very much needed today. But I liked even better his talks about personal responsibility. He quoted St. Jerome, that every house should have a "Christ's room" for our brother who was in need. That "the coat which hangs in one's closet belongs to the poor." Living in tenements as I had for years I had found many of the poorest practicing these teachings.

But of course it was getting out a labor paper which caught my imagination, popularizing the teachings of the Church in regard to social matters, bringing to the man in the street a Christian solution of unemployment, a way of rebuilding the social order.

Peter brought up the idea of the paper the first time I met him and he kept harping on it, day after day. He told me I needed a Catholic background, and he came day after day with books and papers and digests of articles which he either read aloud or left with me to read.

It was impossible to be with a person like Peter without sharing his simple faith that the Lord would provide what was necessary to do His work.

House of Hospitality

THE CATHOLIC WORKER

The Catholic Worker was financed like the publications of any radical "splinter group." If we had had a mimeograph machine, it would have been a mimeographed paper. But we had nothing but my typewriter, so we took our writing to a printer, found out it would cost $57 to get out 2,500 copies of a small, eight-page sheet the size of *The Nation*, and boldly had it set up. There was no office, no staff, no mailing list. I had a small paycheck coming in for the research job which I was just finishing; two checks were due for articles I had written, but these were needed to pay overdue rent and light bills. Father Joseph McSorley, the Paulist, paid me generously for a small job of bibliography which I did for him; the late Father Ahearn, pastor of a Negro church in Newark, gave me ten dollars; Sister Peter Claver gave me one dollar which someone had just given her. Those were our finances. We took that first issue of the paper into Union Square that May Day and sold it for one penny a copy to Communists and trade-unionists.

Jubilee

THE FIRST HOSPICE

So far three beds are all that have been obtained although fifteen are needed. We also have four blankets, two of them donated by a woman the members of whose family are unemployed, save for one son who is working for ten dollars a week. She washed the blankets herself and sent them down to the office with prayers for the success of the new venture. Another woman, unable to afford to buy things herself, canvassed among her friends until she found one who voluntarily brought ten sheets and pillow slips. Another one of our readers sent in two sheets, another sent curtains and a blanket, and she is the mother of a large family and could well use them herself.

The winter is on us and we can wait no longer. Even without furniture we have opened the doors. We will borrow blankets for the time being and use those of the editors. They can roll themselves in coats and newspapers, which are said to be very warm, though we are sure they are also very noisy. However, we hug to ourselves the assurance that all these things, such as blankets, will be added unto us, so we are not dismayed. Come to think of it, there are two rugs on *The Catholic Worker* floor which, if energetically beaten out, will serve as covers.

Christ's first bed was of straw.

Seventh issue of The Catholic Worker

REFLECTIONS OF CHILDREN

Teresa, aged seven, is very much around the office these first cold days. Since *The Catholic Worker* has moved to the store downstairs, there is ample room for another assistant and her little desk.

She likes even better than sitting at a desk to crawl under the furniture coverings of a set of chairs and sofa the young woman rack-tender at the Paulist Church sent down as a contribution to our office furniture. There, ensconced in her tent with her little friend Freddy Rubino, I heard her talking the other day.

"There now," she said, "you have committed a mortal sin, and you haven't got God in your heart anymore."

Freddy is two years younger than herself. Freddy had a few minutes before kicked his mother in the shins and had called her a pig and generally scandalized the neighborhood, though everyone should have been accustomed to witnessing these scenes at least once a day.

Teresa's reproof made Freddy indignant. "He is so there," he insisted. "He's right there."

"No, there's a devil there now."

"I don't want a devil there. I want God there. He is there."

"Well, all you have to do is say you're sorry and it will be all right."

So that was settled.

House of Hospitality

EARLY COMMUNION

The conversation proceeded thus:

"There are no ghosts. Really there aren't," said Teresa.

"But there are spirits," the little girl from upstairs said.

"God is a Spirit and that's enough," Teresa decided.

I was reminded of a story Mother Clark up at the Cenacle of St. Regis had told me of a little girl who was being instructed for her first Holy Communion. They were asking her what a spirit was and when she could not answer they started asking her questions.

"Has a spirit got eyes or hair?"

"Has a spirit arms or legs?" And so on.

She agreed that a spirit had none of these things but she finally said brightly:

"But a spirit has feathers!"

Thank God for Pope Pius X who urged early Communion. He was the one who said that it was sufficient for a child to know the difference between her daily food and the heavenly food she would receive.

I know that if anyone started asking Teresa any questions she would not be able to answer them. She has an aversion to answering questions. My only knowledge of her spiritual processes is through her conversations, either with other children or with me. She will volunteer information, but she will not have it drawn from her by direct questioning.

House of Hospitality

SCAVENGER HUNT

A scavenger hunt is the latest game of "Society." A hilarious pastime, the *New York Times* society reporter calls it, and describes in two and one half columns the asinine procedure of several hundred society and literary figures, guests at a party at the Waldorf-Astoria, surging forth on a chase through the highways and byways of Manhattan Island. "The scavenger's hunt of last night brought an enthusiastic response even from persons whose appetites for diversion are ordinarily jaded. The hunt was a search through the city streets for a ridiculously heterogeneous list of articles."

Any morning before and after Mass and straight through the day there is a "scavenger hunt" going on up and down 15th Street outside the windows of *The Catholic Worker* and through all the streets of the city. People going through garbage and ash cans to see what they can find in the way of a heterogeneous list of articles. The *Times* does not state what these things were, but probably the list was made up of something delightfully and quaintly absurd such as old shoes, bits of string, cardboard packing boxes, wire, old furniture, clothing and food.

If the several hundred guests at the Waldorf had to scavenge night after night and morning after morning, the hunt would not have had such an enthusiastic response.

House of Hospitality

29

HUMAN DIGNITY

One day last summer, I saw a man sitting down by one of the piers, all alone. He sat on a log, and before him was a wooden box on which he had spread out on a paper his meagre supper. He sat there and ate with some pretense of human dignity, and it was one of the saddest sights I have ever seen.

House of Hospitality

OUR LARGE FAMILY

And now of course, there is our House of Hospitality. Ours, of course, is like a large family and when the women come to us they come for an indefinite stay. Some of them have been with us for the past four years. We have no rules, any more than the average family has, and we ask no questions. Many of the women have come to us so exhausted by poverty and insecurity that it has taken them months to recover. There are others who will always be victims of shattered nerves, and incapable of holding down any job. Many of them try to help us and participate in the work around the house. Whatever co-operation they give is voluntary.

House of Hospitality

LITTLE MIRACLES

Our lives are made up of little miracles day by day. That splendid globe of sun, one street wide, framed at the foot of East 14th Street in early morning mists, that greeted me on my way out to Mass was a miracle that lifted up my heart. I was reminded of a little song of Teresa's composed and sung at the age of two.

"I'll sing a song (she warbled)

Of sunshine on a little house

And the sunshine is a present for the little house."

Sunshine in the middle of January is indeed a present. We get presents, lots of them, around *The Catholic Worker* office. During the holidays, a turkey, a ham, baskets of groceries, five pounds of butter, plum puddings, flannel nightgowns and doll-babies, sheets, wash rags and blankets descended on us. There was even the offer of a quarter of a moose from Canada, but we didn't know where we could put it, so we refused it.

House of Hospitality

EMPTY CASH BOX

But now our cash box is empty. We just collected the last pennies for a ball of twine and stamps and we shall take a twenty-five-cent subscription which just came in to buy meat for a stew for supper. But the printing bill, the one hundred and sixty-five dollars of it which remains unpaid, confronts us and tries to intimidate us.

But what is one hundred and sixty-five dollars to St. Joseph, or to St. Teresa of Avila either? We refuse to be affrighted. (Though of course the printer may be, "oh, he of little faith!")

Don Bosco tells lots of stories about needing this sum or that sum to pay rent and other bills with and the money arriving miraculously on time. And he too was always in need, always asking, and always receiving.

House of Hospitality

BASIC COWARDICE

Oh the basic cowardice and inhumanity of man! I remembered how when I was a little girl, another child and I had once been chased around our doll carriages by a fierce dog, and caught at and nipped until our dresses had been torn to ribbons. And I remembered how people witnessing this miserable sight, in their own fear, had not come out to help. We welcomed the policeman who rescued us and I could have kissed his hands with gratitude — those hands guilty perhaps in their turn of other brutalities.

House of Hospitality

INTERNATIONAL HOUSEHOLD

We are an international household. Yesterday afternoon Peter brought in his Armenian friend, Mr. Minas, and asked if we could put up a bed for him. We have the apartment next door as well now, so we got a camp cot to put up in the kitchen after the meetings are over in the evening. Teresa and I each had two blankets, so I took one off each bed for him — one for under and one for over — since a camp cot has no mattress. Now we sit down to table, American, French, Irish, Polish, Jew, Lithuanian, Italian and American.

As for the meetings held every night now, there are all nationalities there too — Ukranian, Spanish, Italian, German, Belgian, Swiss, English, Scotch, Irish, Russian, Negro, French, Lithuanian, Jewish and now — Armenian.

House of Hospitality

DIFFICULTIES

A long day full of difficulties. A priest called up and said he was sending over a young woman who had threatened to kill herself. She had already made one attempt, he said she told him, and she was without work and without shelter, having been put out of her room early that morning. We talked to her, gave her breakfast, some clothes and sent her up to the House of Hospitality.

House of Hospitality

SOUP

And speaking of food, Peter Maurin arrived in from the country after an absence of four weeks. Discussing economics, he displayed his grocery and newspaper bills for the month — $9.

Peter is in favor of a big pot on the stove and a continual supply of vegetable soup, constantly renewed from day to day — an idea shared by both Don Bosco and the I.W.W.'s.

After supper we went out to pushcart market and bought a large pot for 79 cents, a ten-quart one, and while the Workers' School is in session, we shall dine on soup.

House of Hospitality

MEETINGS

The meeting was crowded to the doors. Later in the evening a drunken man came in and listened for a while open-mouthed, and then got up, waving his hand in farewell.

"I've listened and I've listened," he said, "but never once have I heard the name of the Mother of God mentioned." And he went disconsolately out of the door.

If Harry Crimmins had been there, his great devotion to the Blessed Mother would have impelled him to rush out after the poor creature and walk the streets with him all night talking of the Blessed Virgin. But as it was the old man got away before anyone could say a word to him.

Another man came up after the meeting and said, "This is one of the worst evenings I have ever spent; how in the world do you stand it?"

House of Hospitality

WORKERS AND SCHOLARS

Following Peter's ideas, we are trying to make the workers into scholars and the scholars into workers. So we take whoever comes to us as sent by God and do not believe in picking and choosing. If we start eliminating then there is no end to it. Everyone wishes to eliminate someone else. In a group of people living together more or less in community, grievances always pile up which change from day to day and from month to month. Even if we had only picked "intellectuals," young students and propagandists, there would be dissensions and grave differences of opinion. Tom and Dorothy are more at home with the scholars and wish to concentrate more on propaganda. As it is, most of the money is spent on food and shelter and not much is left for the paper and for pamphlets.

But Peter and I feel that the work is more important than the talking and writing about the work. It has always been through the performance of the works of mercy that love is expressed, that people are converted, that the masses are reached.

House of Hospitality

LEARNING PRAYERS

"The way you learn new prayers," Teresa told me, "is just to say them over and over night and morning every day for a while. I like learning new ones so you must teach me some."

Her favorite just now is an ejaculatory prayer, which she says comes to her mind often during the day. "By thy holy pitrinity and by thy Immaculate Conception, purify my body and sanctify my soul."

I gather that the peculiar word in the first phrase means "maternity" and I try to change the prayer for her but she is fond of it the way it is. She is only eight, but quite set in her ways, and if a Sister says a thing, it is so, regardless of what my opinion may be.

The "new" prayer we are learning now is the Song of the Three Children, very fitting to say down here on the beach where there is not only sand and sea, but field and woodland; where there is not only the odor of sweet grass and clover, but the salt smell of seaweed and the pleasant odor of decaying sea life.

House of Hospitality

APPEARANCES

A few weeks ago, I went over to St. Zita's to see a Sister there
and the woman who answered the door took it for granted that
I came to beg for shelter. The same morning I dropped into the
armory on Fourteenth Street, where lunches are being served
to unemployed women, and there they again motioned for me
to go into the waiting room, thinking that I had come for food.
These incidents are significant. After all, my heels are not run
down — my clothes are neat — I am sure I looked averagely
comfortable and well cared for — and yet it was taken for
granted that because I dropped into these places, I needed help.
It shows how many girls and women, who to the average eye
look as though they came from comfortable surroundings, are
really homeless and destitute.

House of Hospitality

41

WHAT WE MUST DO

Let us do the same thing [the Communists do]. Let us canvass blocks, factories, schools, form groups to study, not Marxism, but the encyclicals of the Popes — the writings of the Church on social questions as well as on the liturgy. The two should go together. There should be daily Mass, a community act, as well as the individual work which we must each do. We believe in the Communion of Saints; we know that in the act of the Mass we are associated with a great body, the Church militant, the Church suffering, the Church triumphant.

House of Hospitality

LENIN

Not long ago I read the life of Lenin by his widow. She wrote of a meeting which was held in Paris not so many years ago when twenty or so people attended, and she wrote glowingly of what a splendid meeting it was. Lenin was an exile and gathered his few followers around him wherever he was, and he and his wife thought their meeting of twenty — the usual number we have on these hot summer evenings — a goodly gathering.

And now, not so many years after, this man has taken possession of one hundred and sixty millions of people, one-sixth of the globe, and has established his rule, his dictatorship of the proletariat, and the people revere him as their saint.

And our youth dares to be discouraged, with Christ as its leader, with the Church at its back — its wealth in writings, the very deeds and virtues of its saints to draw upon — and wishes for numbers, for demonstrations, for something to do!

House of Hospitality

RESOLUTION

Our prayer for the new year is that the members may be "mutually careful one for another."

House of Hospitality

POOR WORN FEET

I'd like to have everyone see the poor worn feet, clad in shoes that are falling apart, which find their way to *The Catholic Worker* office. A man came in this rainy morning and when he took off one dilapidated rag of footwear, his sock had huge holes in the heel and was soaking wet at that. We made him put on a dry sock before trying on the pair of shoes we found for him, and he changed diffidently, there under the eye of the Blessed Virgin on the bookcase, looking down from her shrine of Christmas greens. But his poor, red feet were clean. Most of the men and women who come in from the lodging houses and from the streets manage cleanliness, with the help of the public baths. I heard of one man who washed his underwear in the public baths and sat there as long as he could in that steam-laden, enervating atmosphere until it was not quite too wet to put on again. For the rest, it could dry on his skin. Not a pleasant thought in bitter weather. Many of the men do this, he said.

House of Hospitality

FRANCISCAN SPIRIT

Franciscan spirit grows hereabouts. Last night Mr. Minas, who is devoted to our black cat, was discovered washing her chest with my washrag and drying her with my towel and then anointing her with a warming unguent for a bad cough! It is good I discovered him in the act. Then Big Dan, our chief-of-staff on the streets of New York (he sells the paper, either on Fourteenth Street or in front of Macy's every day), took one of my blankets to cover the old horse who helps us deliver our Manhattan bundles of papers every month. He is truly a *Catholic Worker* horse, Dan says, and when they go up on Fifth Avenue and pass St. Patrick's Cathedral, the horse genuflects!

House of Hospitality

DEMOCRATIC CARDINAL

Mary Sheehan has been a faithful saleswoman on Fourteenth Street too. One of her sallies was reported to me recently. A Communist passing by started cursing the Cardinal. "Why, he gets drunk every Saturday with his housekeeper!" he said, hoping to get a rise out of Mary.

"And doesn't that just show how democratic he is." Mary retorted.

House of Hospitality

PHYSICAL WORK

The workers try to become white-collar workers and abandon working with their hands, and the scholars spend their time in work and have no time to study except by grabbing it. So much time must be given to the physical details of life — cleaning beds, kitchens, garbage cans, toilets. It is endless, and it seems to take such a large proportion of time. The majority of people have no machines — dishwashers, cleaners, tractors. Most of the physical work of our existence still has to be done with the hands.

House of Hospitality

GREGORIAN CHANT

Last night the Liturgical group of Campions sang Vespers and Compline. They sang and sang and could not stop. The truckmen in the garage at the back of the house, the police in the station house across the street, were overwhelmed with plain chant.

Tina, our Trotskyite friend, came in to say that "yodeling is an indispensable part of every movement." Out in the Middle West and in the South the strikers sang hymns as they picketed their factories. Even while they were being clubbed, the Communists last month up in front of the 47th Street station house sang Communist songs.

It is good to see Gregorian a part of *The Catholic Worker* movement.

House of Hospitality

THE DIRTY POOR

Most of the time when people talk of efficiency and organization, they are thinking of order, outward order. What they are really criticizing is our poverty, the fact that we spend money for food instead of for paint and linoleum. We are crowded as the poor are, with people sleeping in every available corner. We have no separate room for the clothes that come in; they are packed in boxes around the dining room and hung in one hall closet and in another closet off the dining room. We are often dirty because so many thousands cross our thresholds. We are dirty ourselves sometimes because we have no hot water or bath, because we have not sufficient clothes for changes — even because we are so busy with the poor and the sick that it is hard to take time to journey to the public baths to wash.

House of Hospitality

RIGHTEOUS WRATH

I am reminded of St. Teresa who said, "The devil sends me so offensive a bad spirit of temper that at times I think I could eat people up."

I'm glad that she felt that way, too. St. Thomas said there is no sin in having a righteous wrath provided there is no undue desire for revenge.

House of Hospitality

STRIKE ACTION

When we participate in strikes, when we go out on picket lines and distribute leaflets, when we speak at strike meetings, we are there because we are reaching the workers when they are massed together for action. We are taking advantage of a situation. We may not agree that to strike was the wise thing to do in that particular case. We believe that the work of organization must be thorough before any strike action occurs, unless indeed the strike is a spontaneous one which is the outcome of unbearable conditions.

House of Hospitality

PICKETING ST. JOSEPH

We picketed St. Joseph this past month, when we were sending out an appeal — asking him to take care of our temporal necessities, as he had to take care of the temporal necessities of the Blessed Mother and the Infant Jesus during those long hidden years at Nazareth. It was a peaceful and loving picketing, the crowd of us taking turns to go to the church and there, in the presence of Christ our Leader, contemplate St. Joseph, that great friend of God, and Protector of His Church. One of the girls in St. Joseph's house, when we announced the picketing at the breakfast table, wanted to know, very startled, whether she would have to carry a sign.

House of Hospitality

DISTRIBUTING LITERATURE

Tonight ten of us went up to Madison Square Garden to distribute a few thousand papers before and after one of the Communist meetings which are held there every week. The Garden holds twenty thousand and is always packed to the doors. There is always a crowd who cannot get in.

"What's the idea of distributing literature to that gang of Reds?" one of our friends wanted to know.

And we reply, that if one person of all those twenty thousand who throng the Garden is to the slightest degree moved by anything he finds in *The Catholic Worker,* we will have considered it a good night's work. We heard of one man who was brought back to the faith last month through *The Catholic Worker,* and that one bit of news was enough to make us intensify our efforts.

House of Hospitality

ENCYCLICALS

This month I've been reading the Encyclicals of the Holy Father as I've gone about town on the subway and the elevated. They are the best kind of spiritual reading because they are directed to us now, at the present time, for our present needs. The Encyclical on labor is perhaps the best known, but they are all pertinent, deep and searching in their analysis of the present day and our conduct at this time.

Peter Maurin likes Leo XIII's on St. Francis of Assisi best of all. It calls all the faithful to the practice of voluntary poverty during this materialistic age when Catholics are tainted as well as everyone else. I like the one on St. Francis de Sales, telling how he preached against heresy even when his whole congregation walked out on him; how he distributed literature, tramping through the fields and mountains in his search for souls, sleeping in the snow and the cold, the love of God warming him all the time.

House of Hospitality

A CHRIST ROOM

Part of the House of Hospitality has moved down to Easton. As we keep explaining, our idea of hospitality means that everyone with a home should have a guest room. Two women who help us with the paper and who are interested in our ideals, have moved into tenement apartments on Mott Street and use their spare rooms for those in need of hospitality. One of the striking stewardesses is staying in one apartment, and another woman temporarily out of employment is staying with our friend in the other.

House of Hospitality

NECESSITY FOR SMALLNESS

We emphasize always the necessity of smallness. The ideal, of course, would be that each Christian, conscious of his duty in the lay apostolate, should take in one of the homeless as an honored guest, remembering Christ's words:

"Inasmuch as ye have done it unto the least of these, ye have done it unto me."

The poor are more conscious of this obligation than those who are comfortably off. I know of any number of cases where families already overburdened and crowded, have taken in orphaned children, homeless aged, poor who were not members of their families but who were akin to them because they were fellow sufferers in this disordered world.

House of Hospitality

COMPLINE

While I was at the convent I thought of how we said Compline at Mott Street.

When Margaret beats on a pan lid at 6 p.m. that means supper and the redoubled beating means that Peter Maurin is downstairs holding up the eating by a discussion. He is probably in the middle of making a point.

When the pot lid resounds at seven, that means Compline and we are sorry to say that the gong has to be supplemented by one of the dish washers poking his head in various rooms where more discussions are going on to shout, "All set!"

We are always trying to explain why we say Compline instead of the rosary.

The two great commandments are to love God and to love our brothers. When we are praying the official prayers of the Church, uniting in praise, we are loving God. And because we are praying together, we are loving each other. Some may say this doesn't follow. But just the same, we know that when we are united together in the community room in this evening prayer, we are conscious of a Christian solidarity. As members of the Church, we are united to the whole Church. We are united with Christ Himself who is head of the Mystical Body. We may not do it very well, our poor efforts may be feeble, our hearts may not be right, but the will is there, and united with Him we partake of His merits. He is the only one who can pray right, and we are praying with Him so our prayer is effective. Then too, we are united with each other, and we benefit by all the merits and graces of our brethren.

House of Hospitality

58

THE FAMILY

The first unit of society is the family. The family should look after its own and, in addition, as the early Fathers said, "Every home should have a Christ room in it, so that hospitality may be practiced." "The coat that hangs in your closet belongs to the poor." "If your brother is hungry, it is your responsibility."

February, 1945

SACRAMENT OF DUTY

In a way of course, taking care of your own, children and grandchildren, is taking care of yourself. On the other hand there is the sacrament of duty as Father McSorley calls it. There is great joy in being on the job, doing good works, performing the works of mercy. But when you get right down to it, a work which is started personally often ends up by being paper work — writing letters, seeing visitors, speaking about the work while others do it. One can become a veritable Mrs. Jellyby, looking after the world and neglecting one's own who are struggling with poverty and hard work and leading, as such families with small children do these days, ascetic lives. There are vigils, involuntary ones, fasting, due to nausea of pregnancy for instance, but St. Angela of Foligno said that penances voluntarily undertaken are not half so meritorious as those imposed on us by the circumstances of our lives and cheerfully borne.

On Pilgrimage

THE CHRISTIAN LIFE

The Christian life is certainly a paradox. The teaching of St. John of the Cross (which was for beginners, he said) is of the necessity for detachment from creatures; of the need of travelling light through the dark night.

Most of us have not the courage to set out on this path wholeheartedly, so God arranges it for us.

It would seem to the unthinking that mothers of children, whether of one or a dozen, are intensely preoccupied with creatures: their little ones, food, clothing, shelter, matters that are down to earth and grossly material such as dirty diapers, dishes, cooking, cramming baby mouths with food, etc. Women's bodies, heavy with children, dragged down by children, are a weight like a cross to be carried about. From morning until night they are preoccupied with cares but it is care for others, for the duties God has given them. It is a road once set out upon, from which there is no turning back. It is their way to glory and salvation.

On Pilgrimage

POVERTY OF FAMILIES

When I talk about poverty I do not mean destitution which is something quite different. Nor do I want to "talk poor mouth" as my mother used to say. I talk about the poverty of young people newly married, the girl without a dowry, the young man without anything, either a team of horses, or a sum of money, or a truck, to make a start in life. Mainly because their parents were also poor, or had many children, or at any rate no tradition of the parents' duty to educate and start their children in life. I read somewhere that according to Jewish law, if a father did not give his son a trade, that son did not owe his father support in his old age. St. Paul, a scholar, was a tentmaker, a weaver of goats' hair.

On Pilgrimage

HANDCRAFTS

One way of combating the system, Tamar says, is to stop buying
the products of our machine world, our capitalist industrial
society. If you want a rug, make it. If you want rosary beads,
or crucifix, make them. The crudest samples of your own work
will very often be better than that which you can buy. Ade lives
in Newport and Tamar stayed with her and her family for a
year. Part of her education was to shop intelligently for the
family groceries. How to buy and cook cheap cuts of meat,
how to bake and churn, keep a kitchen fire going, how to care
for small animals in a back yard, how to letter and bind a book.
For a Christmas present Tamar lettered a chapter from Eric
Gill's *What Is Christianity?* and bound it in sailcloth for me.

On Pilgrimage

HABIT OF WORK

Peter Maurin, founder of a movement, a man of vision, changing the course of thought of thousands, has talked for fifteen years of crafts, of manual labor. Yet how many have tried to acquire a skill, either to carpenter, lay brick, make shoes, tailor or work at a forge? Many, thinking of the family, the need for a home and space and food, have turned to the farm. But a farmer needs capital, and many skills, besides the *habit of work*. A village economy could use doctors, barbers, veterinarians, bakers, launderers, canners, builders, shoemakers, tailors, etc. Not to speak of weavers. Every man, doing some particular job, could be an artist too and from his work, beauty would overflow. As Peter always put it, there would be a synthesis of cult, culture and cultivation.

On Pilgrimage

FOOD IN THE OLD TESTAMENT

How much there was about food in the Old Testament! Adam
raised food for himself and Eve, and did it with pleasure. After
the fall of Adam, ploughing and seeding and harvesting,
earning one's daily bread either as a husbandman like Cain or
a shepherd like Abel, was a difficult and painful affair. Sacrifices of food were offered to the Lord, whether of beasts, or
of bread and wine — food because it represented our life —
what we live by. We offered our lives to the Lord. We also lust
after food as Esau did when he sold his birthright for a mess of
pottage. The Israelites complained of their food in the desert
and yearned after the flesh pots of Egypt even with the bondage
and slavery it entailed, even though the Lord fed them bread
from heaven and water from the Rock, food that had every
delight and taste.

Who can forget the widow's cruse of oil which was never
diminished; Ruth gleaning in the corn; Daniel and his three
companions living on "oats, peas, beans and barley corn"; and
the meal that was served Daniel in the lions' den by the prophet
Habacuc? St. Bonaventure said that after the long fast of our
Lord in the desert, when the angels came to minister to Him,
they went first to the Blessed Mother to see what she had on
her stove, and got the soup she had prepared and transported
it to our Lord, who relished it the more because His Mother
had prepared it. Of course.

On Pilgrimage

FOOD IN THE NEW TESTAMENT

I have always meant to go through the New Testament to see how many times food is mentioned, how many times Christ dined, supped, picnicked with His disciples. He healed St. Peter's mother-in-law and she rose to serve them. He brought the little girl back to life and said, "Give her to eat." He broiled fish on the seashore for His apostles. Could it possibly be that Mary was less solicitous for the happiness and comfort and refreshment of others?

It is part of a woman's life to be preoccupied with food. She nurses her child; she has nourished him for nine long months in her womb; it is her grief if her breasts fail her; she weeps if her child refuses to eat. Her work as food provider is her pleasure and her pain, pain because of the monotony and because right now the cost of food has gone up one hundred percent.

On Pilgrimage

THE LITTLE WAY

When a mother, a housewife, asks what she can do, one can only point to the way of St. Therese, that little way, so much misunderstood and so much despised. She did all for the love of God, even to putting up with the irritation in herself caused by the proximity of a nervous nun. She began with working for peace in her own heart, and willing to love where love was difficult, and so she grew in love, and increased the sum total of love in the world, not to speak of peace.

December, 1968

67

WOMEN'S INSTINCT

I guess women know these things instinctively. A woman's anguish is turned into joy when a child is born into the world. Henri Daniel-Rops once asked, after the crucifixion, when the apostles and disciples all hid in fear, what did the women do? "They went on about the business of living, pounding the spices in which to embalm the body." They went on about the business of living. There are the three meals to get, the family to care for, "the duty of delight" that Ruskin spoke of, for the sake of others around us who are on the verge of despair. Who can say there is no delight, even in a city slum, especially in an Italian neighborhood where there is a pot of basil on the window sill and the smell of good cooking in the air, and pigeons wheeling over the roof tops and the tiny feathers found occasionally on the sidewalk, the fresh smell of the sea from the dock of the Staten Island ferry boat (five cents a ride)?

Peter Maurin used to say, "Man is spirit, woman is matter," and I knew what he meant by this obscure Thomistic utterance. Woman is close to the material things of life, and accepts them, this integration of soul and body and its interaction. St. Teresa of Avila said once that if her nuns were melancholy, "feed them steak!" She reminded us too — "All things are passing."

May, 1969

IMPATIENCE

The trouble is, people do not work in peace and quiet. They bustle, like Martha. They give the impression of being impatient and fussy.

January, 1945

EVERYONE IS CHRIST

What mother ever considers the ugliness of cleaning up after her baby or sick child or husband? These are things not mentioned by critics. But to the saints everyone is child and lover. Everyone is Christ.

June, 1944

SEXUAL LOVE

Sometimes the Scriptures seem full of one great love song in the midst of tragic and gory history. Sexual love is seen as a mighty force in man, his creative power. Man is co-creator with God, made in the image and likeness of God. What a gift of oneself then is this celibacy that is embraced by clergy and religious, and by laymen — in some cases willingly, in other cases unwillingly. When marriages are broken up by death and separations the unwilling celibate (since there is no element of self-will in it) has the power to offer this great gift to God — no trivial gift this sex, so often used in life as a plaything.

September, 1965

HIGHEST SPIRITUALITY

The point I want to make is that a woman can achieve the highest spirituality and union with God through her house and children, through doing her work which leaves no time for thought of self, for consolation, for prayer, for reading, for what she might consider development. She is being led along the path of growth inevitably. But she needs to be told these things, instructed in these things, for her hope and endurance, so that she may use what prayer she can, to cry out in the darkness of the night.

Here is her mortification of the senses.

Her eyes are affronted by disorder, confusion, the sight of human ailments, and human functions. Her nose also; her ears tormented with discordant cries, her appetite failing often; her sense of touch in agony from fatigue and weakness.

Her interior senses are also mortified. She is alone with her little ones, her interest adapted to theirs; she has not even the companionship of books. She has no longer the gay companions of her youth (their nerves can't stand it). So she has solitude, and a silence from the sounds she'd like to hear, conversation, music, discussion.

Of course there are consolations and joys. Babies and small children are pure beauty, love, joy — the truest in this world. But the thorns are there of night watches, of illnesses, of infant perversities and contrariness. There are glimpses of heaven and hell.

On Pilgrimage

72

FEAR

One can get by if one's wants are modest. One can withdraw from the factory, refuse to make munitions, airplanes, atom bombs. In sections like this [West Virginia, 1947] rent is ten a month, sometimes even five dollars, and there are empty houses. But city people are afraid, afraid of the country, afraid of the dark, afraid to be alone, afraid of the silence. They confess to it. And I remember myself, once, as a little girl, wandering out along the beach down at Fort Hamilton, sitting at the edge of a swamp and listening to the cicadas on a hot summer day, and suddenly being overcome by fear. Even as a little child of six I often awakened in the dark and felt the blackness and terror of non-being. I do not know whether I knew anything of death, but these were two terrors I experienced as a child, a terror of silence and loneliness and a sense of Presence, awful and mysterious.

On Pilgrimage

73

WE ARE CHRISTIAN PACIFISTS

The position of *The Catholic Worker* remains the same. We are Christian pacifists and try to follow the counsels of perfection. Man is a creature of body and soul and as such has a supernatural destiny as well as a part to play in this temporal order. We firmly believe that our stand makes for the common good, basing our view on the philosophy of history which Peter Maurin as our teacher presents to us. We may suffer for this faith, but we know that this suffering will be more fruitful than any words of ours.

January, 1941

TO OPPOSE WAR

There are so many who hate war and who are opposed to peacetime conscription who do not know what they can do, who have no sense of united effort, and who will sit back and accept with resignation the evils which are imposed upon us. This is not working for God's will to be done on earth as it is in Heaven. This is accepting the evils in the world as inevitable and looking toward Heaven as a haven, a "pie in the sky" attitude. God did not make the evils, but man in his misuse of his free will.

October, 1940

SPIRITUAL WEAPONS

All our talks about peace and the weapons of the spirit are meaningless unless we try in every way to embrace voluntary poverty and not work in any position, any job, that contributes to war, not to take any job whose pay comes from the fear of war, of the atom bomb. We must give up our place in this world, sacrifice children, family, wife, mother, and embrace poverty, and then we will be laying down life itself.

On Pilgrimage

REFUSE TO MAKE WAR

We say frankly, that we wish indeed the workers would lay down their tools and refuse to make the instruments of death. We wish that they were so convinced of the immorality of modern wars that they would refuse to make the instruments of those wars.

April, 1941

DANGEROUS TIMES

There is so much fear and distraction these days over the state of the world — there is sadness in the Pope's Christmas message, in articles, in letters, in all endeavors. And yet surely, "all times," as St. Teresa said, "are dangerous times."

We may be living on the verge of eternity — but that should not make us dismal. The early Christians rejoiced to think that the end of the world was near, as they thought. Over and over again, even to the Seventh Day Adventists of our time, people have been expecting the end of the world. Are we so unready to face God? Are we so avid for joys here, that we perceive so darkly those to come?

On Pilgrimage

PENANCE

I could not help thinking how little penance we have done these last years, how little mortification, how little dying to self, which is what mortification is. To mortify is to put to death, to do violence to oneself. "You have not yet resisted unto blood," St. Paul said. "Without the shedding of blood there is no salvation." Blood means *life* in Biblical terms. Some years ago I saw a man die of a heart attack before my eyes, and his skin became like wax as the blood stopped moving in the veins and seemed to drain back to the heart.

If our cause is a mighty one, and surely peace on earth in these days is the great issue of the day, and if we are opposing the powers of darkness, of nothingness, of destruction, and working on the side of light and life, then surely we must use our greatest weapons — the life forces that are in each one of us. To stand on the side of life we must give up our own lives. "He who would save his life must lose it."

September, 1965

LESS EATINGS

And now Advent is upon us and we must begin to fast. We read (in a Hearst paper!), picked up from a subway seat, that the Holy Father is beginning a week's vigil for peace, spending the time in prayer and fasting. Rabbis and ministers, of New York City, according to the story, are joining with him in prayer. It gives one a great sense of loyalty and devotion to our Holy Father when we hear of his storming Heaven with his supplications. We want to join him, to add our prayers and sacrifices to his. Last Lent our priest in the Precious Blood Church around on Baxter Street was enjoining us all to fast. "Too much eatings, and too much drinkings!" he told us sternly. And too little prayer.

December, 1939

HERO WORSHIP

It is true that much hero worship is misplaced, exaggerated, even hysterical. But it is also true that war makes the common soldier realize the tremendous adventurous capabilities of man. Farm boys, laborers, the man in the street is suddenly trained to fly the ocean, to risk his life daily. What is cheered as remarkable in peacetime is expected of the multitude in time of war. Gruelling hours, constant work, in medical corps, in kitchen police, often heroic sacrifice. (These are times when by compulsion soldiers are expected in theory to practice the counsels of poverty, obedience and chastity. If you speak openly of the tolerated and organized brothels and saloons situated near the huge camps you are traitorous. These things are not supposed to enter into the picture of our heroes' lives.) And if the physical capabilities of our citizens are tapped to such a degree, then what about the spiritual? They have been consistently neglected, and neglected, too, by our churchmen.

April, 1942

THE HOLY FATHER

What about our Holy Father as one of the heroes of the day? Do we wear buttons to remind us of our spiritual leader? Do we hang on his words with breathless interest and greet his every utterance with joy? Do we examine what he says, weigh his words, follow his leadership? Do we meditate on what he has said, do we ponder it prayerfully, do we try to serve under his banner as valiant soldiers of Christ? If we did there would be far more pacifists today, far more conscientious objectors.

April, 1942

POVERTY IS LICE

Our poverty is not a stark and dreary poverty, because we have the security which living together brings. But it is that living together that is often hard. Beds crowded together, much coming and going, people sleeping on the floor, no bathing facilities, only cold water. These are the hardships. Poverty means lack of paint, it means bedbugs, cockroaches and rats and the constant war against these. Poverty means body lice. A man fainted on the coffee line some months ago and just holding his head to pour some coffee between his drawn lips meant picking up a few bugs. Poverty means lack of soap and Lysol and cleansing powders.

September, 1939

LOVE OF BROTHER

Love of brother means voluntary poverty, stripping one's self, putting off the old man, denying one's self, etc. It also means non-participation in those comforts and luxuries which have been manufactured by the exploitation of others. While our brothers suffer, we must be compassionate with them, suffer with them. While our brothers suffer from lack of necessities, we will refuse to enjoy comforts. These resolutions, no matter how hard they are to live up to, no matter how often we fail and have to begin over again, are part of the vision and the long-range view which Peter Maurin has been trying to give us these past years. These ideas are expressed in the writings of Eric Gill. And we must keep this vision in mind, recognize the truth of it, the necessity for it, even though we do not, can not, live up to it. Like perfection. We are ordered to be perfect as our heavenly Father is perfect, and we aim at it, in our intention, though in our execution we may fall short of the mark over and over. St. Paul says, it is by little and by little that we proceed.

On Pilgrimage

PATIENCE OF THE POOR

I certainly don't think the poor ever get used to cockroaches, bedbugs, body lice, fleas, rats and such like vermin that go with poverty. They merely endure them, sometimes with patience, sometimes with a corroding bitterness that the comfortable and the pious stigmatize as envy. Someone asked Peter once why God had created bedbugs, and he said: "For our patience, probably."

February, 1945

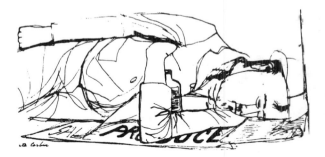

UNPOPULAR FRONT

The Catholic Worker is controversial also in its attitude to the war on poverty. To attack poverty by preaching voluntary poverty seems like madness. But again, it is direct action.

"The coat that hangs in your closet belongs to the poor." And to go further, "If anyone takes your coat, give him your cloak too." To be profligate in our love and generosity, spontaneous, to cut all the red tape of bureaucracy! "Open your mouth and I will fill it," says the Lord in the Psalms. The more you give away, the more the Lord will give you to give. It is a growth in faith. It is the attitude of the man whose life of common sense and faith is integrated.

To live with generosity in times of crisis is only common sense. In the time of earthquake, flood, fire, people give recklessly; even governments do this.

September, 1964

LACK OF LEADERSHIP

Once when some Quaker friends came to visit us at the farming commune at Easton, they told us we had two great assets in our work on the farm — one, our poverty, and two, our lack of leadership. We were much startled to hear this and much encouraged. It is true that our poverty should force us to use the means at hand, whether it be stone or earth for houses, if wood is lacking. It is true that our poverty should force us to work for food and clothing. It is true that when there is no educated, strong, and spiritual leadership, each man has to depend on himself.

February, 1944

KNOWLEDGE OF THE POOR

How few there are who are reaching these men, these unemployed, these destitute, to bring them Catholic social teachings, some idea of the correlation of the material and the spiritual, so that they can indeed begin to realize that they are creatures of body and soul. How great a need there is to build up many little centers where men gather together and discuss these things and get these ideas moving. Patience, contentment with the little way, hard work, obscurity and poverty, the knowledge of the poor which results in the love of the poor, these are what is needed.

May, 1940

UNWORTHY POOR

God is on the side even of the unworthy poor, as we know from the story Jesus told of His Father and the prodigal son. Charles Peguy, in *God Speaks,* has explained it perfectly. Readers may object that the prodigal son returned penitent to his father's house. But who knows, he might have gone out and squandered money on the next Saturday night; he might have refused to help with the farm work, and asked to be sent to finish his education instead, thereby further incurring his brother's righteous wrath, and the war between the worker and the intellectual, or the conservative and the radical, would be on. Jesus has another answer to that one: to forgive one's brother seventy times seven. There are always answers, although they are not always calculated to soothe.

February, 1968

FAULT OF THE POOR

Over and over again we meet good people who are under the delusion that there is little poverty in the United States, that we are all enjoying a high standard of living, and when presented with such pictures as these they can scarcely believe them. "It must be their own fault. They are shiftless, they drink, they go to moving pictures and do not save their money. Everyone can get a job these days." These are the comments they make.

April, 1943

INSECURITY

Baron von Hugel writes that we should have interests on different levels to relieve the tension in our lives. And only the other day I saw an article in the evening paper on knitting as a tranquillizer. The study of sea weeds and other aspects of shore life, and knitting too have given me great relief in these times of stress. I almost forget the holes that are being dug around us, the imminent collapse of our building, and come to myself with a start and go out hunting again, investigating stoves and plumbing fixtures for the loft. "They," holy mother the city, have even taken our good kitchen stove, and we must buy another.

Anyway, we repeat, we may have a loft, a day shelter, the bare bones of a place, but there is no place yet to sleep. We are looking for a miracle in the way of an apartment, three or four apartments in the same house, within our means. A miracle indeed. St. Therese, St. Anthony, St. Joseph (to go back through time) will be looking out for us, we are sure. And our guardian angels!

November, 1958

POVERTY FREES

It is voluntary poverty which needs to be preached to the comfortable congregations, so that a man will not be afraid of losing his job if he speaks out on these issues. So that pastors or congregations will not be afraid of losing the support of rich benefactors. A readiness for poverty, a disposition to accept it, is enough to begin with. We will always get what we need. "Take no thought for what you shall eat or drink — the Lord knows you have need of these things."

July, 1964

SLUM LANDLORD

How strange a situation for us to be in — to be speaking sympathetically of this man! And how terrible it is to see that I myself am in the same category, a convicted criminal, under suspended sentence for being a slum landlord This is in connection with the trouble we had in 1956 which led to us remodeling our St. Joseph's house at the cost of $24,000 only to be told two years later we had to move out to make way for a subway. There were eleven violations in our house which led to my conviction. At the plea of my lawyer, Judge Nichols thundered that if we were a charitable group, all the worse for us because these poor people we helped could not move out!

What very strange encounters come about through the practice of the works of mercy. What strange lessons we learn through this hard way, of loving our enemy, in the class war which is basic in the world today, very much a part of all the cold war which is going on between the rich and the poor.

January, 1959

WE WERE NOT ASKED

No one asked us to do this work. The mayor of the city did not come along and ask us to run a bread line or a hospice to supplement the municipal lodging house. Nor did the Bishop or Cardinal ask that we help out the Catholic Charities in their endeavor to help the poor. No one asked us to start an agency or an institution of any kind. On our responsibility, because we are our brother's keeper, because of a sense of personal responsibility, we began to try to see Christ in each one that came to us. If a man came in hungry, there was always something in the ice box. If he needed a bed and we were crowded, there was always a quarter around to buy a bed on the Bowery. If he needed clothes, there were our friends to be appealed to, after we had taken the extra coat out of the closet first, of course. It might be someone else's coat but that was all right too.

September, 1942

TRUE CENTERS OF HOSPITALITY

Our Houses of Hospitality are scarcely the kind of houses that Peter Maurin has envisioned in his plan for a new social order. He recognizes that himself, and thinks in terms of the future to accomplish true centers of Catholic Action and rural centers.

Our houses grew up around us. Our bread lines came about by accident; our roundtable discussions are unplanned, spontaneous affairs. The smaller the house, the smaller the group, the better. If we could get it down to Christian families, we would be content. Ever to become smaller — that is the aim.

September, 1942

WORKS OF MERCY

The works of mercy are works of love. The works of war are works of the devil — "You do not know of what spirit you are," Jesus said to his disciples when they would call down fire from heaven on the inhospitable Samaritans. This is to look at things in the large context of modern war. But as for the hostilities in our midst, the note of violence and conflict in all our dealings with others — everyone seems to contribute to it. There is no room for righteous wrath today. In the entire struggle over civil rights, the war which is going on in which one side is non-violent, suffering martyrdoms, every movement of wrath in the heart over petty hostilities must be struggled with in order to hold up the strength of the participants.

July, 1964

PRESENT HELP

The greatest help we have received spiritually this last month has come in the shape of a little quarterly, *Jesus Caritas,* a publication of the Charles de Foucauld Association. The theme of the number is *The Gift of Friendship* and the best of the articles in it are the two of Fr. Rene Voillaume, whose volume of conferences *Seeds of the Desert* I have referred to before in my column.

Several times those poignant lines of St. Vincent de Paul are quoted — "It is only by feeling your love that the poor will forgive you for the gifts of bread." He elaborates on this in his description of the special mission of the Little Brothers in a lecture "delivered extempore at Sao Paulo, Brazil," to the Little Brothers there.

He points out how the Church has led in the works of mercy, in education down through the ages, and how many of these works are being taken over by the state when the need is so vast.

January, 1959

TENDERLY TO THE POOR

Within *The Catholic Worker,* there has always been such emphasis placed on the works of mercy, feeding the hungry, clothing the naked, sheltering the harborless, that it has seemed to many of our intellectuals a top-heavy performance. There was early criticism that we were taking on "rotten lumber that would sink the ship." "Derelict" was the term used most often. As though Jesus did not come to live with the lost, to save the lost, to show them the way. His love was always shown most tenderly to the poor, the derelict, the prodigal son, so that he would leave the ninety-nine just ones to go after the one. We are plunging deeper and ever deeper into the problem when we put aside these most workable ways for the time being, to stress the mutual aid of a war-torn society. It is, in a way, emergency work, the vanguard work we are doing. Others will come along, and have come along, to go forth from this school of action to work in the adult education movement, the credit union movement, the cooperative movement, to start new schools, to work as teachers, writers, etc., apostles in new fields, wherever God leads them, wherever they find their vocation.

February, 1959

IMMEDIATE SOLUTION

I was reminded of Abbé Pierre and his work when a woman told me of going to the garbage cans of the chain stores and retrieving damaged goods, soap powder which had gotten wet, canned goods dented or with labels stained. You can feed many hungry people by such means.

The immediate solution will always be the works of mercy. We are commanded by Jesus Himself in the 25th chapter of St. Matthew to perform them. But there is more study to be done, a long-range view to take, to understand how far-reaching works of mercy can be.

Vinoba Bhave asked the rich to give to the poor and the poor to give to each other. Many villages in India now hold all things in common. His Bhoodan movement has been going on since Gandhi's death. He walks all over India, is walking as I write, a prophet in our times. He has converted the leading Socialist of India. Nehru is trying to work out some of his program.

The absolutist begins a work. Others take it up and try to spread it.

In this country too the final solution will be the commune, but how it will be brought about is in God's hands. He may permit a bloody revolution.

March, 1959

NOT MANY CLOTHES

A cold rainy May, and now June is beginning the same way. Coats and sweaters are still necessary. The men that come in on the line need shoes and socks, coats and shirts. Not many clothes are coming in right now. The last two days it has rained. I asked one young fellow how he got that way, and he said he had missed his ship, been "rolled," had slept in doorways and eaten on the "line" while waiting for his ship to come back to port. Every day come in those who have fallen among thieves and been robbed. Some with cracked heads, black eyes, some with hospital pallor.

June, 1945

PICKETING — A WAY OF MERCY

To go on picket lines to protest discrimination in housing, or to protest the draft, is one of the works of mercy, which include "rebuking the sinner, enlightening the ignorant, counselling the doubtful." But I confess I always do these things with fear and trembling. I loathe the use of force, and I remember how Peter used to react to violence. On one occasion when two men fought in the office over on Charles Street he threatened to leave the work forever if it ever happened again. In a collection by Fedotov on *Russian Spirituality,* there is the story of St. Sergius, who left his monastery for two years rather than impose his authority by force. On another occasion years ago at the Easton farm, one man knocked down another over a dispute about an egg (it is horrible to think of people fighting physically over food), and for the rest of the summer Peter ate neither eggs nor milk in order that others might have more. That was his idea of justice.

On Pilgrimage

COMMUNAL ASPECTS

To bring back the communal aspects of Christianity — this is part of Peter's great mission. "A heresy comes about," he said, "because people have neglected one aspect of the truth or distorted it." Communism is just such a heresy. We have neglected the communal aspect of Christianity; we have even denied that property was proper to man. We have allowed property to accumulate in the hands of the few, and so a denial of private property has come about, ostensibly for the sake of the common good. St. Thomas says a certain amount of goods is necessary to lead a good life.

February, 1944

A MOVEMENT

People come to join us in "our wonderful work." It all sounds very wonderful, but life itself is a haphazard, untidy, messy affair. Unless we can live simply, unquestioningly, and solitary, one might say, in the midst of a mob, then we cease to be a personalist. The more we live with people in a community, the more we must look to ourselves and regard the beam in our own eyes. The more we live with a babbling crowd, the more we must practice silence. "For every idle word we speak we will be judged."

February, 1943

IMPORTANCE OF COMMUNITY

Theodosius emphasized the importance of community life, I read today, and one of his monks declared that a "Lord, have mercy on us" prayed from the heart collectively by the community is of greater religious value than the whole psalter said alone in one's cell. His monastery had a hospital for the sick and the disabled, they had a hospice for travelers, and every Saturday a cartload of food was sent down to the city jail.

November, 1963

COMMUNITY OF BREAD

We must minister to people's bodies in order to reach their souls. We hear of the faith through our ears, we speak of it with our mouths. The Catholic Worker movement, working for a new social order, has come to be known as a community which breaks bread with brothers of whatever race, color or creed. "This is my body," Christ said at the Last Supper, as He held out bread to His apostles. When we receive the Bread of life each day, the grace we receive remains a dead weight in the soul unless we cooperate with that grace. When we cooperate with Christ, we "work with" Christ, in ministering to our brothers.

October, 1940

TRUE LOVE

True love is delicate and kind, full of gentle perception and understanding, full of beauty and grace, full of joy unutterable. Eye hath not seen, nor ear heard, what God hath prepared for those who love Him.

And there should be some flavor of this in all our love for others. We are all one. We are one flesh in the Mystical Body, as man and woman are said to be one flesh in marriage. With such a love one would see all things new; we would begin to see people as they really are, as God sees them.

We may be living in a desert when it comes to such perceptions now, and that desert may stretch out before us for years. But a thousand years are as one day in the sight of God, and soon we will know, as we are known. Until then we will have glimpses of brotherhood, in play, in suffering, in serving, and we will begin to train for that community, that communion, that Father Perrin talked so much about in his story of the workman priest in Germany.

On Pilgrimage

RETREAT HOUSES

And where are we going to learn to pray? Where are we going to learn to use these spiritual weapons? The only answer that we can see is in retreat houses, where we can spend eight days every year and monthly days besides, in silence and in receiving instruction. It is certainly a dream for the future — a retreat house by the sea. The immensity of the sea will lead us so naturally to worship and adore the greatness of God. A retreat house with farming commune attached where food can be raised for all the retreatants, who will be workers and poor people from our bread lines, mothers from the slums. There would almost have to be a nursery attached where these mothers could leave their children for a week. Here at such a retreat house, mothers could receive such instruction as that which is given by the Ladies of the Grail at their courses in Wheeling, Illinois.

And where are the priests and where are the teachers to give these retreats for the integrated Christian life? God certainly will send them to us.

September, 1943

HOLY WEEK

During Holy Week we celebrated the Last Supper, setting the long tables in the refectory with unleavened bread and wine, bitter herbs and wild garlic with a dressing in a big dish in the middle of the table, and we tried to get lamb to roast, but could not, so we took what was said to be beef instead. There were about fifteen of us from the farm at table, and there was just a morsel of meat each, just enough to give us an idea of what the Passover feast was like. Next year we shall have a roast lamb, we hope, from the farm itself. During the meal we read the story of the Last Supper.

April, 1945

COMMUNITY OF THE WOUNDED

People are always thinking we have accomplished what we are holding up as an ideal, and the simple ones who come to us keep wondering why we have not already built that kind of society where it is easier for men to be good, as Peter Maurin expressed it. It is a wonder, with all their expectation and disappointment, they do not go away, but bad as we are, it is worse outside, someone said; or "though I am unhappy here, I am more unhappy elsewhere," someone else said. And so we are really not a true communal farm, a true agronomic university, but a community of need, a community of "wounded ones" as one girl, who came to us from a state hospital, expressed it. I myself have often thought of our communities as concentration camps of displaced people, all of whom want community, but at the same time want privacy, a little log cabin of their own, to grow their own food, cultivate their own gardens and seek for sanctity in their own way. This kind of sanctity of course has for most of us as little validity as the sense of well-being of the drug addict. "Man is not made to live alone," as we are told in the Book of Genesis.

May, 1964

TOTAL DEDICATION

I am pretty well convinced, what with my experience of the CW activities of the last twenty-five years, that God wants the total dedication of those who are working together with us, to voluntary poverty and the works of mercy. Which would mean that the money earned should go into a common purse, that all feeling of independence would be given up and our sense of the Mystical Body so deepened that we would always be working with the idea — "Let your abundance supply their want." That doesn't mean that aside from *The Catholic Worker* and its particular program of action, such small groups would not be very successful indeed, a healthy cell within the old society, or rather a new society within the shell of the old. A few failures, a few falls! There is always the work of helping each other up again and starting again. Chesterton said: "It is not that Christianity has not been tried. It has been tried and found difficult." People give up too easily.

February, 1959

CLERGY VS. LAITY

Of all hostilities one of the saddest is the war between clergy and laity.

July, 1964

LOVE AND LOYALTY

The non-Catholic does not realize what a relationship of love and loyalty there is between the layman and the priest, the priest and bishop. In all the great events of one's life, birth, marriage and death, and for the unmarried the confirming of their vocation. For the times of sin and sickness, there is absolution and anointing, and at the moment of death, the holy oils and the prayers of priest and the people. It is our Faith which lends strength and dignity to our paltry and tragic lives. "In Thy hand are strength and power and to Thy hand it belongs to make everything great and strong."

July, 1964

CRITICAL SPIRIT

If only more seminarians spoke out, even if the seminaries were emptied! (It is said the seminaries of France were half-emptied because of the Algerian War, which went on for so long.) If more young priests spoke out while they continued to work hard and continued to "be what they wished the other fellow to be," as Peter Maurin put it — what happy results might not be brought about.

But often the critical spirit results in desertions, from Church and priesthood and seminary, and I suppose that is what the hierarchy fears. We have plenty of experience of the critical spirit and have seen the ravages that can be wrought in family and community. We have had many a good worker leave because he could not stand the frustrations, because "those in charge" did not throw out troublemakers, or *force* people to do better. The critical spirit can be the complaining spirit too, and the murmurer or complainer does more harm than good.

If we could strive for the spirit of a St. Francis, and it would be good to read his life and struggles, we would be taking a first step, but it is only God himself who can make a saint, can send the grace necessary to enable him to suffer the consequences of following his conscience, and to do it in such a way as not to seem to be passing judgment on another, but rather to win him to another point of view, with love and with respect.

July, 1964

113

STRONG MEAT OF DOCTRINE

When a man, black or white, reaches the point where he recognizes the worth of his soul (what does it profit a man if he gain the whole world and suffer the loss of his soul?) — when he begins to realize what it means to be a child of God, a son, an heir also, the sense of his own dignity as a child of God is so great that no indignity can touch him, or discourage him from working for the common good.

It is for this that our shepherds are to be reproached, that they have not fed their sheep these strong meats, this doctrine of men divinized by the sacraments, capable of overcoming all obstacles in their advance to that kind of society where it is easier to be good.

Let Catholics form their associations, hold their meetings in their own homes, or in a hired hall, or anyplace else. Nothing should stop them. Let the controversy come out into the open in this way.

But one must always follow one's conscience, preach the Gospel in season, out of season, and that Gospel is: "All men are brothers."

This teaching is contained in all the work of the Confraternities of Christian Doctrine. It just needs to be applied.

July, 1964

LAYMEN LEAD

Bishop O'Hara of Kansas City once said to Peter Maurin, "You lead the way — we will follow." Meaning that it was up to the laity to plough ahead, to be the vanguard, to be the shock troops, to fight these battles without fear or favor. And to make the mistakes. And that has always been my understanding. This business of "asking Father" what to do about something has never occurred to us. The way I have felt about Los Angeles is that the lay people had to go ahead and form their groups, "Catholics for Interracial Justice," form their picket lines, as they are only now doing, and make their complaints directly, to priest and cardinal, demanding the leadership, the moral example they are entitled to.

How can any priest be prevented from preaching the gospel of social justice in the labor field and in the interracial field? One can read aloud with loud agreement those messages from the encyclicals, which are so pertinent to the struggles which are being carried on. One can tell the Gospel stories in the light of what is happening today. Do the poor have the Gospel preached to them today? Do we hear that resounding cry, "Woe to the rich!" Do we hear the story of the rich man sitting at his table feasting while the poor sat at the gate with neither food nor Medicare? How many priests have read Fr. Regamey's *Poverty* or Shewring's *The Rich and the Poor in Christian Tradition?*

July, 1964

DIRECT ACTION

Bernanos said, "Hell is not to love any more." Righteous wrath and indignation is usually not loving. Jesus said to love our enemies.

But to speak of the whole problem on the natural plane, it seems to me an enormous waste of energy to direct our attacks against the hierarchy instead of attacking the problem of the poverty of the Negro, his joblessness, his homelessness, the insult and injury which is inflicted on him. It is a temptation of the devil, a diversion of our energies. Direct action would be to rent and sell to Negroes in our own neighborhoods, or to take in a Negro family as an immediate work of mercy, to find work, to start an industry, a pilot project — in other words, to use one's energies and imagination. Some actions would be fruitful and some would raise persecution and as much of a hullabaloo as the letter-writing on the West Coast. Direct action, rather than the indirect action of asking why the hierarchy behaves as it does, would be more to the point.

September, 1964

WE MUST BEGIN

We have to begin to see what Christianity really is, that "our God is a living fire; though He slay me yet will I trust Him." We have to think in terms of the Beatitudes and the Sermon on the Mount and have this readiness to suffer. "We have not yet resisted unto blood." We have not yet loved our neighbor with the kind of love that is a precept to the extent of laying down our life for him. And our life very often means our money, money that we have sweated for; it means our bread, our daily living, our rent, our clothes. We haven't shown ourselves ready to lay down our life. This is a new precept, it is a new way, it is the new man we are supposed to become. I always comfort myself by saying that Christianity is only two days old (a thousand years are as one day in the sight of God) and so it is only a couple of days that are past and now it is about time we began to take these things literally, to begin tomorrow morning and say, "Now I have begun."

April, 1965

REVERENT HOMAGE

I am a traditionalist, in that I do not like to see Mass offered with a large coffee cup as a chalice. I suppose I am a romantic too, since I loved the Arthur legend as a child and reverenced the Holy Grail and the search for it. I feel with Newman that my faith is founded on a creed, as Rev. Louis Bouyer wrote of Newman in that magnificent biography of his.

"I believe in God, the Father Almighty, Creator of heaven and earth. And of all things visible and invisible, and in His Only Son Jesus Christ, our Lord."

I believe too that when the priest offers Mass at the altar, and says the solemn words, "This is my body, this is my blood," that the bread and the wine truly become the Body and Blood of Christ, Son of God, one of the Three Divine Persons. I believe in a personal God. I believe in Jesus Christ, true God and true man. And intimate; oh how most closely intimate we may desire to be. I believe we must render most reverent homage to Him who created us and stilled the sea and told the winds to be calm, and multiplied the loaves and fishes. He is transcendent and He is immanent. He is closer than the air we breathe and just as vital to us. I speak impetuously, from my heart, and if I err theologically in my expression, I beg forgiveness.

March 1966

TO STUDY HISTORY

Peter Maurin says the way to study history is through Bible history and the history of the Church. We will then have a philosophy of history, a perspective. Certainly a study of the Old Testament in these times helps one to the long view, makes one think in the light of eternity.

My library, as I travel, is made up of missal, Bible, short breviary, the life of Janet Erskine Stuart, her travels and letters, and the last number of *Land and Home,* Mcnsignor Ligutti's rural life journal. Whenever I read the Bible on the bus, someone asks me if I am a Seventh Day Adventist or a Jehovah's Witness!

June, 1942

COURAGE

It seems to me that we must begin to equal a little bit the courage of the Communists. One of the ways my Communist friends taunt me is by saying, in effect: "People who are religious believe in everlasting life, and yet look how cowardly they are. And we who believe only in this life, see how hard we work and how much we sacrifice. We are not trying to enjoy all this and heaven too. We are willing to give up our life in order to save it."

April, 1968

BRIDE OF CHRIST

There is plenty to do, for each one of us, working on our own hearts, changing our own attitudes, in our own neighborhoods. If the just man falls seven times daily, we each one of us fall more than that in thought, word and deed. Prayer and fasting, taking up our own cross daily and following Him, doing penance, these are the hard words of the Gospel.

As to the Church, where else shall we go, except to the Bride of Christ, one flesh with Christ? Though she is a harlot at times, she is our Mother. We should read the Book of Hosea, which is a picture of God's steadfast love not only for the Jews, His chosen people, but for His Church, of which we are every one of us members or potential members. Since there is no time with God, we are all one, all one body, Chinese, Russians, Vietnamese, and He has *commanded us to love one another.*

"A new commandment I give, that you love others as *I have loved you"* not to the defending of your life, but to the laying down of your life.

A hard saying.

"Love is indeed a harsh and dreadful thing" to ask of us, of each one of us, but it is the only answer.

January, 1967

WORLD OF PARADOX

A Jewish convert, who had been making a retreat with us at Maryfarm, said some weeks after, "It is hard to live in the upside-down world of the Gospels." Truly it is a world of paradoxes, giving up one's life in order to save it, dying to live. It is voluntary poverty, stripping oneself even of what the world calls dignity, honor, human respect.

September, 1945

VIGIL OF CHRIST

A German woman doctor, who spent a year in a concentration camp for refusing to sterilize epileptics, said that one form of torture inflicted was to turn blinding lights into the cells so that the women could not sleep. This is to be keeping vigil with Christ. To keep vigil voluntarily is to be sharing his pain of the world, this agony of the Mystical Body. Insomnia may be keeping vigil.

January, 1944

TO BE A PERSONALIST

To be a personalist does not mean to be a quietist. No matter if it seems hopeless, "we must hope against hope." "In peace is my bitterness most bitter." These are hard words to understand, but we can at least remember that all times are in the hand of God.

On Pilgrimage

IT IS TOO LATE

A priest we know who does not like our emphasis on distribution, decentralism, or whatever one wishes to call it, said one time, "It is too late for anything but love." That sounded good to many poeple. But that same priest was going about his business having his church repaired $20,000 worth.

On Pilgrimage

MAY DAY DISTRIBUTION

Every year, every May Day, friends and fellow workers from coast to coast have taken bundles of papers out to May Day Parades, out to the parks, and distributed. It is spring and we are scattering seeds. It is not for us to think of the harvest — our job is to do the sowing. Is the ground poor, is it hard and stony, is the crop to be choked by weeds? We will water it with our prayer. Throughout the country priests, monks and nuns in their powerhouses will generate the heat and light and power to enable us to carry on the work.

May, 1941

PERFECT JOY

Peter Maurin, visiting our Buffalo house one time, showed his face inside the door and was so greeted: "Come back at five and have soup with the rest of the stiffs." And then the comment, "One of those New York bums came in this afternoon and said he was from the New York house."

One of the friends of the work, in laughing at the incident that evening, said: "Where did you go, Peter?" "I went to see *The Grapes of Wrath*."

On Pilgrimage

STABILITY

One of the vows the Benedictines take is *stability*. And there is such wandering today, from job to job, from home to home. Most people want a settled place, but economic circumstances make it hard.

On Pilgrimage

MANUAL LABOR

We should write more about manual labor. It's another one of the foundation stones of the work, of the social edifice we are trying to build. Manual labor, voluntary poverty, works of mercy, these are means of reaching the workers and learning from them, and teaching them. Besides inducing cooperation, besides overcoming barriers and establishing the spirit of brotherhood (besides just getting things done), manual labor enables us to use our body as well as our hands, our minds. Our bodies are made to be used, just as they are made to be respected as temples of the soul. God took on our human flesh and became man. He shared our human nature. He rose from the dead and His disciples saw the wounds in His hands, His feet and His side. They saw His body, that it was indeed a body still. He was not a disembodied spirit. We believe in the resurrection of the body, free from fatigues, from pain and disease and distortion and deformities, a glorified body, a body transfigured by love. All those are reasons for respecting the body, and using it well, not neglecting it by disuse.

May, 1941

MARTYRDOM

"A new commandment I give unto you, that you love others as I have loved you," that is, to the *laying down* of one's life. The commandment of love, which is binding on us all, in Old Testament and New, was finally heard by Peter, once the denier, and by Franz Jagerstatter in the second World War. And by how many others through the ages whose histories have never been written? Our God is a hidden God, and such stories are hidden too in the lives of the saints.

We read in the life of Theophane Venard in Vietnam of how he considerately shed his clothes before his head was chopped off so that the executioner who was paid for his deed with them would not be receiving blood-stained garments. Such was his love for his enemies, remembering Jesus' words, "Father, forgive them, for they know not what they do." We think of the martyrs of Uganda, Protestant and Catholic, when we read the history of Africa and her exploitation.

July, 1965

PERSONAL LOVE

It is not love in the abstract that counts. Men have loved a cause as they have loved a woman. Men have loved the brotherhood, the workers, the poor, the oppressed — but they have not loved man, they have not loved the least of these. They have not loved "personally." It is hard to love. It is the hardest thing in the world, naturally speaking. Have you ever read Tolstoi's *Resurrection*? He tells of political prisoners in a long prison train, enduring chains and persecution for their love of their brothers, ignoring those same brothers on the long trek to Siberia. It is never the brother right next to us, but brothers in the abstract that are easy to love.

April, 1941

TROUBADOURS OF CHRIST

More than ever am I convinced that the solution lies only in the Gospel and in such a leader as St. Francis. Peter Maurin has been talking these past two years of recruiting troubadours of Christ. More and more am I convinced that together with our purely material efforts of building up hospices and farming communes we need these fellow travellers with the poor and the dispossessed to share with them their poverty and insecurity and to bring them the reminder of the love of God.

May, 1940

SOWING TIME

"The only way to have more time," says Father Lacouture, "is to sow time." In other words, to throw it away Just as one throws wheat into the ground to get more wheat. It must have seemed madness to throw that first wheat away — but more wheat sprang up a hundredfold.

So each day, start out by saying, there is plenty of time. And so to discard time, to throw it to the winds, to disregard all the work there is to do, and go sit in the presence of the Blessed Sacrament for an hour, to divest oneself of these accursed occupations — all in order to reap time, for those things which are necessary. Press Day is a very good day for that.

February, 1941

LITTLEST ONES

I often think that our Lord must have been terribly bored with the disciples very often, humanly speaking. Certainly, He wasn't picking out brilliant, accomplished, pleasing personalities with whom to live. Isn't it in today's epistle where the mother of James and John wanted the best place for her two sons? So even the relatives were hanging on to see what they could get out of the situation. He certainly had to get away from them every now and then and do a lot of praying.

They say a mystic is someone who is in love with God, again using that comparison as the kind of love we should feel. This is one of the most absorbing problems of all the work, this relationship we have to all those around us, the tie that holds us all around the country together.

June, 1941

134

ALL THE WAY TO HEAVEN

We are not expecting utopia here on this earth. But God meant things to be much easier than we have made them. A man has a natural right to food, clothing and shelter. A certain amount of goods is necessary to lead a good life. A family needs work as well as bread. Property is proper to man. We must keep repeating these things. Eternal life begins now. "All the way to heaven is heaven, because He said, 'I am the Way.'" The Cross is there of course, but "in the Cross is joy of spirit." And love makes all things easy. If we are putting off the old man and putting on Christ, then we are walking in love, and love is all that we want. But it is hard to love, from the human standpoint and from the divine standpoint, in a two-room apartment. We are eminently practical, realistic.

On Pilgrimage

SUMMING UP

We have heard this same word, "a band-aid for a cancer," from Boston and Milwaukee and even from the Australian bush within the last year. Perhaps it is only those words of the Gospel about the corporal works of mercy, which in a way include the spiritual works of mercy, that has kept us going all these years. We are commanded over and over again by Jesus Christ Himself to do these things. What we do for the least of these, we do for Him. We are judged by this. It is the picture of the last judgment in the 25th chapter of Matthew. Actually, we here at *The Catholic Worker* did not start these soup lines ourselves. Years ago, John Griffin, one of the men from the Bowery who moved in with us, was giving out clothes, and when they ran out he began sitting down the petitioners to a hot cup of coffee, or a bowl of soup — whatever we had. By word of mouth the news spread, and one after another they came, forming lines (during the Depression) which stretched around the block. The loaves and fishes had to be multiplied to take care of it, and everyone contributed food, money and space. All volunteers who come, priests and people, nuns and college students, have worked on that line and felt the satisfaction of manual labor, beginning to do without themselves to share with others, and a more intense desire to change the social order that left men hungry and homeless. The work is as basic as bread. To sit down several times a day together is community and growth in the knowledge of Christ. "They knew Him in the breaking of bread."

December, 1969

WORK OF A JOURNALIST

This book is the work of a journalist who writes because it is her talent; it has been her means of livelihood and it is sent out with the hopes that it will sell, so that the bills will be paid. We write also to help support the work which we are doing, because we have a very big family, ranging in age from the infants at the Tivoli farm to those who are advanced in age. It is written most personally because I am a woman who can write no other way. If it is preaching and didactic in parts, it is because I am preaching and teaching and encouraging myself on this narrow road we are treading.

"Life," said St. Teresa, "is but a night spent in an uncomfortable inn, crowded together with other wayfarers."

There are bills to pay at an inn of course, and they are one of the reasons which led me to send the manuscript forth, in the care of St. Joseph, patron of all families. May God bless it, and you who read it.